This Grace of Light

This Grace of Light

Patrick T.R. Gray

Hidden Brook Press

First Edition

Hidden Brook Press
www.HiddenBrookPress.com
writers@HiddenBrookPress.com

Copyright © 2009 Hidden Brook Press
Copyright © 2009 Patrick T.R. Gray

All rights for poems revert to the author. All rights for book, layout and design remain with Hidden Brook Press. No part of this book may be reproduced except by a reviewer who may quote brief passages in a review. The use of any part of this publication reproduced, transmitted in any form or by any means, electronic, mechanical, photocopied, recorded or otherwise stored in a retrieval system without prior written consent of the publisher is an infringement of the copyright law.

This Grace of Light
by Patrick T.R. Gray

Editor – Eric Winter
Cover Art – Patrick T.R. Gray
Layout and Design – Richard M. Grove
Cover Design – Richard M. Grove

Typeset in Garamond

Printed and bound in Canada

ISBN – 978-1-897475-34-8

Library and Archives Canada Cataloguing in Publication

Gray, Patrick T. R.
 This grace of light / Patrick T.R. Gray.

Poems.
ISBN 978-1-897475-34-8

 I. Title.

PS8613.R3883T45 2009   C811'.6   C2009-903548-0

For Cathy Carlyle,
bringer of joy and contentment

Table of Contents

— This Grace of Light - *p.1*
— The Thing About Cedars - *p.2*
— With My Father at the Symphony - *p.3*
— Why I Am As I Am - *p.5*
— The Power of the Weak - *p.6*
— The Sweet Men - *p.8*
— The Tallness of Trees - *p.10*
— Finding the Tao - *p.11*
— The Sounds of Ice - *p.12*
— Thrust the Dark, Blue Blade - *p.13*
— In One Another's Eyes - *p.14*
— Benedicta - *p.15*
— Benedictus - *p.16*
— Deprivations - *p.17*
— In This Season - *p.18*
— Shopping with Henriette - *p.19*
— The Return of Grief - *p.21*
— First Snow - *p.22*
— Red - *p.23*
— Snow Angels - *p.24*
— In Canada, a Long-Distance Call - *p.25*
— To Titian - *p.26*
— The Music, but Not Yet the Dance - *p.28*
— Red-Wing - *p.30*
— Spring Gold - *p.31*
— Philodendron - *p.32*
— By Sturgeon Creek - *p.33*

- Charmed Life - *p.34*
- Messages from Beyond - *p.35*
- Under this Enchantment - *p.36*
- You, Too, Contain The Light - *p.38*
- On First Looking Into Pärt's Te Deum - *p.39*
- At Saint Mary Magdalene's - *p.41*
- A Garden, Walled - *p.42*
- This is Where - *p.44*
- Genealogy - *p.45*
- At 87 - *p.53*
- Her Arms - *p.54*
- You Never Know - *p.55*
- The Shadow Children - *p.57*
- Briefing Notes - *p.58*
- Beyond - *p.59*
- Molly - *p.60*
- Ruth - *p.62*
- David - *p.64*
- Cousins - *p.65*
- A Cat's Lament for St. Valentine's Day - *p.67*
- Boad - *p.68*
- Gratuity - *p.69*
- Beyond the Apogee - *p.70*
- It Seems, Then - *p.72*
- Asters - *p.73*

- Acknowledgements - *p.75*
- Biographical Sketch of Author - *p.76*

Introduction

We hear many voices in these poems, from the "triumphant shout" of encroaching waves during the spring melt of lake ice, to the "silent clearing/In the dark cedars, filled with mid-winter light".

Hopkins comes to mind in a celebration of "The tallness of trees,/ Their crowns fan-vaulting/ Into heaven", their bark in the autumn chill "still vibrant/ With descending sap." In a poem addressed "To Titian" the artist's palette is rendered in tones of winter leaves against snow, amusingly "For the highlights you so love ... / The dogwood tangle's spears/ Of irreligious red."

The poems of loss are often very moving, their tone— with some striking exceptions— gentle and restrained. There is a rare scrupulosity in Gray's expression of emotions and moods. At the end of a meditation in "At Saint Mary Magdalene's" that is delicate, tentative, hesitant, he can affirm: "There is transfiguration, / Of a sort, / And a certain kind of peace."

Here are poems we can savour and trust.

> John Unrau, author of *ICED WATER: POEMS*,
> published in 2000
> by Salmon Books, Ireland.

Preface

The sound of poetry being read or sung belongs to my earliest memories, memories of my father's and mother's voices reciting Beatrix Potter, A. A. Milne, and Robert Louis Stevenson. I remember, too, ancient 78rpm recordings of A.A. Milne poems set to music, and played over and over by us children. The sound of Dylan Thomas's magical Welsh voice reading his poems, broadcast by Max Ferguson on his CBC radio show when I was a bit older, moved things to a different plane: here was unashamed poetic language that could not only delight you, but also touch you to the quick. I knew then that, if I were ever to write poetry, I would want it to touch people in something like this way; Thomas's voice is, to this day, never quite silent in my head when I write and read my poems. I hope they succeed in some measure; what I know is that they move me, or I would not write them.

But I only dabbled in the writing of poetry—a few sonnets and such for high school and college journals—until the early 1990s, when upheavals in my life somehow stimulated an urge to write which has, so far, refused to leave me in peace. The present collection represents poems written at and since that time.

Thanks are owed to many without whose encouragement and support I could and would not have persisted in the craft. From my Amherst Island and Kingston days I want to mention particularly Peter Trueman, Grier Owen, Bill Hedges and Lisa Spano. Among my colleagues at York University I am especially grateful to John Unrau for leading me to join the Atkinson Writers at Noon group; he and the other members of that group gave me the opportunity to be a poet among poets, and to hear the encouraging comments we classified, correctly, not as criticism, but as the kindlier "business arising out of the poems." I have been fortunate to move smoothly, on my retirement to Port Hope, from the Atkinson group to the close-to-home Cobourg Poetry Workshop, which has provided me an equally stimulating and nourishing environment. Thanks go to all of its members for making that so.

I reserve a special mention for Eric Winter, a forerunner in the transition from Atkinson to Cobourg, a founder of the Cobourg Workshop, and the one who invited me to join the latter. Eric's wonderful but quiet encouragement was and is all the more valued because it comes from a man possessed of such integrity, such a keen intelligence, and such a high poetic gift.

I am perpetually grateful for the support and love I have received in all things from my four wonderful sons, Trevor, Ben, Tim, Geoff, and their families. Above all, I thank my wife, Cathy Carlyle, to whom this volume is lovingly dedicated.

This Grace of Light

Oh, I would share the heart's leap,
And the eye's high exaltation!
How can I bear, alone,
This grace of light—
The halcyon flash,
Wing upon wing,
Above the waterbrook;
Dark arc of falcon flight
Across a dome of azure;
Gold-crimson epaulettes
Amazing against ebony;
Black crescent, colour's absence
In a yellow blaze of morning?

The Thing About Cedars

The thing about cedars
Is the way they huddle together
In the hollows,
Roots and progeny following,
Unerring,
The water's path,
Encircling it
In their own
Secret
Silence.
Here you may hide
From the wind's frenzy,
And the sun's insistence;
When all else
Is blasted heath,
May sink your feet
Into the dark mould
And draw, slowly,
Your life again
From the mysterious earth.

With My Father at the Symphony

It is a communion ritual:
Dinner at The Spur,
The jostle in the lobby,
The long climb to the second balcony,
Delight, as the orchestra tunes up,
And bliss;
The intermission smoke
On the fire-escape
Above empty, silent streets,
And at the end
The quiet drive home,
Rich with aural memory,
A companionable pee outside the barn
Where we keep the car,
And sleep.

He walked in music,
As others walk in thought,
And music poured from his lips
And fingers.

He died in music,
The music my mother promised
Would be playing to the end,
His last words to me
The words of a song:
"I'm leaving, on a jet plane,
Don't know when I'll be back again."

And now that he is gone
I scarcely know,
When these tears start in my eyes,
This sob catches in my throat,
Whether it is for loss of him,
Or memory,
Or pained astonishment
That such loveliness dares to sound
When he, who loved so well,
No longer lives to hear.

Why I Am As I Am

"Go to your mother", my father pleaded,
Impotent to heal a pain
That was the image of his own—
One child, again, lying at death's door,
The other with a damaged brain—
And I, miraculous,
The strong, the well, the bright,
Went down into the basement
Where she wept.

The Power of the Weak

She sucked,
The legend says,
His life out
Through eyes
She seemed to kiss,
A parody of love.

I think her terrible power
Lay not in strength
But weakness—
He had. She needed.
She could therefore take,
As the nursing child,
Unthinking,
Draws calcium
From the starving mother's bones.

It lay, also, I think,
In his susceptibility
To weakness,
The Red Cross Knight
All eager
To bare his arm
For the transfusion
That would, he fancied,
Share the gift of life,
Not suck away his own.

This is what I,
Who have been kissed
Upon the eyes,
And more than once,
Think.

The Sweet Men

This is about the sweet men,
The ones who,
By good luck,
Or genetic defect,
Escaped.

They love their wives, e.g.
The once-blonde beauty
Whom one of them calls
"The last of the great broads,"
And believes it;
They dance a pas de deux
Without once wishing
It were their solo;
They still enjoy a roll in the hay
With the so-familiar flesh.

They stay on the phone
When their children call.
When they were little,
They rubbed their legs
In the middle of the night,
Or sang the magic songs
That made the darkness safe again.
They saw their sons and daughters
Lose at sports, or school,
And praised them.

They see, now,
Their friends succeed or fail
In marriage, or in business,
Manage only a few words,
Passed off as a joke,
But see that they
Are invited to dinner,
And let their wives do
What men are seldom good at.

They make good sons:
They reassure their fathers
That the air-conditioner
In the retirement home
Is Y2K-compliant,
Or repeat instructions,
With no edge in their voices,
For logging on;
They take their mothers out
For lunch, or for a drive,
Guide the spoon to their mouths,
In the last days,
And hold their hands
When all speech fails.

Their passing is not marked,
As that of their greater,
Troubled brothers is.
It's just that a dapple of brightness
Fades from the world,
Scarce noticed in the chiaroscuro,
And we are less
Against the dark.

The Tallness of Trees

I call no ground true home,
A place where I could dwell
For now, or for eternity,
Whose edges are not marked
By the tallness of great trees—
Sleek-skinned, bronze-budded beech,
Sweet-sap-dripping sugar maples,
Vast-trunked and tulip-branched elms,
Dark hemlocks brooding darkly
Over still, wooded shades—
Foliate pillars,
They enclose
Fit space for habitation
And meditation,
Sacred groves,
The tallness of trees,
Their crowns fan-vaulting
Into heaven,
Giving shape
Even to the transcendent
For those who know
To lift their eyes.

Finding the Tao

There is a trick to it, of course—
You follow the tracks of deer,
Or else the watercourses.
The way opens to the secret places
Of the earth, the silent clearing
In the dark cedars, filled with mid-winter light,
The startling sheets of perfect ice
Yearning aslant towards the distant lake,
The shrike singing, solitary,
To the snowbound land.

I thought, "These are metaphors
For what will be," but found, instead,
Myself as I have been:
My soul a dark clearing
Not empty of, but longing to be fully filled
With light;
My powers icebound, extorted all one way,
Longing in free spate
To exert their not inconsiderable art;
My heart a solitary song.

The future, perhaps, is implicit in the longing
That will find its way,
As the deer will find their way through the brush,
And the streams will find theirs to the lake,
By the lay of the land,
And the bird's song, in due time,
Will find a waiting ear.

The Sounds of Ice

You heard it first in the bays,
Slowly filling with tectonic plates:
A sweet, crystalline tinkle
That is the prelude to silence.

You stood on the imprisoned deep
And felt, rather than heard,
Mysterious, distant/present booms,
As the lake turned in its sleep.

You could, sometimes, break off a piece
And send it for miles across
The newly-refrozen surface,
Could hear a white, unearthly tone,
Some indecipherable message from beyond.

But what you hear now—
What you can not, must not fail to hear—
Is the painful clash of crystal
Against crystal, shard against shard,
And beyond, the triumphant shout of waves.

Thrust the Dark, Blue Blade

Thrust the dark, blue blade between the fields of ice,
Dividing island from mainland with turbulence once more;
Drive the hyacinth up through frozen, recalcitrant earth
To brave the cold and bitter winds of March, of April;
Exile the birds to the north, into the lingering snow,
Set them, male against male, to proprietorial song;
Send the bucks into groves of prickly ash to tear
The velvet in long, bloody strips from violent antlers;
And—for God's sake—let my new life begin!

In One Another's Eyes

There has been time,
And will be time again,
To savour loneliness.
Right now,
Give me the warmth
And press of people:
Give me the affirmation
Of adoration in a student's face,
The glad "hello"
When I call,
The hand on my shoulder,
The hug, the kiss.
Give me too, now,
The cheerful insouciance
Of bodies,
Their warm, animal smells,
Their humid couplings,
Their eating,
And their drinking,
And their making merry.
There may be virtue
In silence,
The strength of the solitary,
But I think we live—
Pack animals that we are—
Not for ourselves,
But for ourselves
In one another's eyes.

Benedicta

"To desire the desiring
Of her own delightfulness,
That is the rebellion of Lilith;
To desire the enjoyment
Of her own delightfulness,
That is the obedience of Eve."

So Freud.
But what did he know
About sex anyway?
Certainly obedience wasn't in it,
For either you or me,
And as for desiring the desiring,
There was hardly time for that.

But enjoyment, now,
There he has a point:
If you desired enjoyment
Of your own delightful self,
Then, O my dear,
You have indeed been blessed.

Benedictus

What I chiefly remember—
Though I forget nothing—
Is the benediction
Of your incandescent smile,
Sanctifying, by its light,
The gifts I gave you,
And blessing, too, the giver
As one possessed of gifts
Worthy the giving.

Deprivations

I step out.
Crisp, autumnal light,
Poured out from the morning sun,
Inhabits the glass-hard air,
My responsive, eager eyes.
The dog steps with me.
At once his nostrils test
The redolent air,
Breathe in the world.
It is rich with the doings,
And the droppings,
Of his kind,
The hair-raising challenges
Of squirrels, and of cats,
And our abominations.
I would not trade with him;
But would he,
Having known superb olfaction,
Settle for our smell-blindness's
Grey in grey?

In This Season

In this season,
It is the light that astonishes,
The cold lending a crispness,
A limpidity,
To the startling gold of leaves
Straggling yet
On trees
Bent by the sharper wind,
Their bark still vibrant
With descending sap;
To dogwoods still proclaiming
Their unrepentant red
Against the resurgent dun.
But most of all
It is the air,
Poured by the sun
From East to West
In bright procession,
That celebrates
The light's last festival
Of deepest,
Confident
Blue.

Shopping with Henriette

It is, no doubt, a mistake
To put together in a car
Two people theologically-trained,
Then send them shopping.
It is, almost, an act
Injurious to the public safety,
As we ritually run the STOP signs,
Deeply engrossed in talk.
(I blame the notorious volatility
Of the German character.)

After the danger come the challenges:
Finding a parking-spot close to the carts;
Separating same from their mutual embrace
(A quarter works better than a fire-hose;
That and a well-aimed karate chop);
Walking the luxuriant piles,
Selecting the choicest samples
Of Italian broccoli-baroque;
Remembering to have each item weighed—
Each purchase here being singular, unique;
The choice of bread—hers, naturally,
Heavy, dense, teutonic,
Mine Italian, or Wonder
(With which, after all, philosophy begins;)
There is, as well, the ethical dimension—
My vegetarian disapproval of her meat,
Her constraint when, nonetheless, I do buy fish.

At last the check-out. Which has chosen well,
And can stand smirking on the other side?
Then self-congratulation at finding the tiny car,
And at our consummate skill in packing it.

Transfiguration of the commonplace.

The Return of Grief

Again the colours pierce
With imperious brightness:
The goldenrod,
Green-tinged,
The luxuriant purple asters,
The sumac candles,
Fruiting Titian-red,
And, oh,
The blue autumnal light!

Quisling colours,
You made a way
For the return of grief.
You brought me forth from shadow
To feel the joy of light
And, in the same heartbeat,
Sorrow broke through
And pierced me:
She is no longer here
To share your benediction;
We live apart
Who should rejoice together.

First Snow

I love this first, soft
Falling of the snow,
(Though you,
Exiled to Winnipeg
For sins unspecified
Of some previous life,
See snow quite differently)
Containing my small world
In swirling canopies of white
Reflecting inwards
A celebratory light,
Whatever lies beyond.
If you were here,
And bundled in my arms,
Would you not, too,
Stand silent,
And receive
These flakes of falling light
As benediction?

Red

Because red is a colour of Christmas;
Because the holly bears a berry,
But not here;
Because red is the colour of blood,
And therefore promises life;
Because red is the colour of fire
'Gainst a cold season;
Because red is for sex, and fast cars,
For the mare's flashing,
And for the flower's deep throat;
Because red stands out vividly
Against the darkening wood;
Because red bears the light;
Because, in the vastness,
The gods are, sometimes, gracious—
Therefore the cardinal.

Snow Angels

Tim makes snow angels
At midnight.
Later,
Seth too is making angels,
Rolling,
Happily ridiculous.

Who is to say
Which has captured best
Those ministers of fire
In Downsview snow?
Do they who attend
The sapphire throne
Think, with Tim-like thoughts,
The Essence all divine,
Or romp, with joyous barks,
Before the path of the Lord?

In Canada, a Long-Distance Call

Here in the warmth of my room,
Lying on the brass bed
In which my father was born
In a pool of light and warmth,
I scarcely hear the snow
Against my window
Swirling whitely down
The whole, deep, frozen distance
Lying between us—

The fisher hunting, methodically,
From tree to tree,
Climbing a few feet,
Sniffing, moving on;
The great grey owl
Punching ferocious claws
Through crusted drifts;
The bear in dreamless sleep
Somewhere beneath the snow;
The unimaginable swell
Of Lake Superior
Swallowing snow's white
In its enormous black;
The wastes of prairie,
Ravaged by unimpeded wind,
Figured in white on white—

And you on your bed, with tea,
Pick up the phone.

To Titian

If you could,
By special dispensation,
Be here—and paint—
You would love most
The sumacs
For their candles,
So opulently red
Against midwinter grey,
And for the flaming swirl
And flare of branch
And trunk,
Defying winter's death
With exultant shapes of life.

You would love, too,
The shadowed, shapely greens
Of winter pines,
Again so like your own velvets,
Folded and draped,
Bright, or dimly dark.

In vain would you search
For your luminous shades of satin blue
Poured across pale flesh
At this dark time of year,
But you would, I trust,
Sense the wonder
Of beeches' glowing skin,
And of winter grasses' browns,

Catching what little light remains
At close of day,
In serried ranks marching across
The anonymity of snow.

And last—
To come full circle—
For the highlights you so love,
I would propose
The dogwood tangle's spears
Of irreligious red.

The Music, but Not Yet the Dance

In the late December air,
Cool and clear as glass,
Two redtails circle
In graceful gyres,
Each
Exulting in its strength,
Its mastery of the heights,
Yet connected to the other,
Across the wind-tides,
By currents of complete attention.
No one,
And least of all myself,
Could mistake
The pas de deux.

Not yet for us:
Each day demands anew
The launching,
All alone,
Against the indifferent air,
The making of such pattern
As one can impose,
In solo flight,
Upon the emptiness.

Unbearable,
This severing
Of bodies made
To inhabit all one space,
Could voice, and thought,
And intuition
Not jump the space between:
Though not yet joined
In movement to one measure,
We, listening, partake,
Deep down,
A single music.

Red-Wing

Still the sun
Beams bright the scarlet.
There is no mistake,
Though March snow
Lies thick around the tree:
You too have noted,
With an expert eye,
The gradual-deepening blue,
Have felt beneath your wing
The thickening buoyancy of air
That I can only savour
In nostrils lifted to the wind,
An animal,
Sensing change.

Malcontents,
We take for blessing
This turning of the wheel,
Accept that flash
Of scarlet light
As invitation
To, again, begin
The lively,
Aching,
Lovely
Dance.

Spring Gold

Where recent snowflakes fell
Against columns of black spruce
You planted years ago,
Forming persistent, shadowed drifts
To metal the way for cutters long-decayed,
I seek your springtime benefaction:
Forsythia, I think, for forcing;
But no, there is none.
Introduced too late from China,
Or did you fear it would not flower here
So far from town?
No, you bequeath me only teasel,
Sober reminder of the flocks you tended,
And, for future plunder,
Tumultuous lilacs
Tumbling down the hill,
Wild Persians, running riot.

I, too, have planted, reckless,
As if it were forever:
Flowerbeds, children, trees,
Ideas, pearls of wisdom, precious insights,
Each in their various soils.
A century past,
Will he pronounce them blessings—
The stranger come to seek
Spring gold amid my ruins?

Philodendron

I know you well enough,
My dendronous love,
Whatever skin you take:
Wearing your favourite colour—
Luminous, vernal green—
As this young poplar;
Or, clad all in beech-silver,
Betraying your sweet eyes
In these bronze-budded shoots;
Or as this lissome, lovely birch
In bridal white,
Moving
With characteristic grace,
And downcast eyes.

Do you think I'd miss
The spread of fingers
In foliate disguise
Against the deepening blue,
Not recognize,
In the confluence
Of limbs and trunk,
Your secret places,
The mysterious darkness
Of your hair
In wild-cherry's blackened bark—
You who inform these woods
As you inform my eyes?

By Sturgeon Creek

Tumescent,
The ancient rivers rise,
Meeting and melding
Over the prostrate land.

For others are the fears—
Assiniboine
Swelling over its banks
And into gardens;
The Red
Sweeping farms away;
Dark waters
Welling
Beneath the fragile city.

We walk
Hand in hand
By Sturgeon Creek,
Exploring,
With ducks and muskrats,
The borderlands of chaos,
More devotees
Than victims
Of Anath and Ba'al
In this
Their sacred congress.

Charmed Life

I have always loved them,
A couple of the sunlight,
Untouched by dark.

There they were,
At his mother's funeral,
Smiling,
Greeting the mourners,
Though the tears stood
In his brother's eyes.
I knew
It was a choice.

And who would not choose
The all-bright
Gold-wove
Garment of their life,
Given the chance?

Though I have worn
A life more somber,
Its wefts of darkness
Mingling warps of light,
I resent nothing
Of their happy choice and chance;
I fear
The turning of the wheel.

Messages from Beyond

The goshawk stalls
In a flap of wings,
Plummets,
For a moment stands
Upon its prey,
Is gone;
Across the rocks
Come the dart
And iridescence
Of a skink
On its mysterious rounds;
In the falling dusk
We hear the splash,
Ominously loud,
Of an unseen fish;
Across the roof
At midnight
A patter,
A leap,
Silence.

We,
The interlopers,
Receive these messages
From beyond,
Barely imagine
What it might imply
To be a native-speaker.

Under this Enchantment

This is where action
And sensation,
Like the motion
Of that metaphysical god,
Are also rest
By being circular,
Endlessly repeated,
Around a central point.

You seem, at least,
Forever:
Wave sound,
And loon call,
Smoke drift,
Immortal blue
Of blueberries richly clustered
Beneath the sun,
Flag flap
At the wind's shift,
Hummingbird flit
From fuchsia
To bergamot.
Rich is the round of life
Under this enchantment.

Who has deserved
Such richly active rest?
And who,
Having joined the dance,
Can fail to turn,
And return,
Until his dancing's done?

You, Too, Contain The Light

I have seen trees
That fill with liquid light
At close of day,
Poured full like glasses
With rich and golden wine.
I have seen flowers
Return to the morning sun
Reflected glory,
Or, lying purple in deep grass,
Glow cool and luminous
When daylight has long gone.

And you,
You, too, contain the light
Within your eyes,
And hide it in your hair,
Reflect its spirit in your voice
Like shards of sunlight
Out of dancing water.
You bring the light
To cloak our shoulders 'round,
To linger in your face
When darkness comes.

On First Looking Into Pärt's *Te Deum*

What we see
Are the hems—
The hints of the hems—
Immeasurably distant,
Of tall, angelic figures
Dancing
With profound solemnity,
Their skirts
The woven reflections
Merely
Of an inconceivable light
About which they move.

What we hear
Are the refracted measures
Of their music—
Arch upon arch of sound
Stretching illimitable,
Rich
And infinite variations
Spun
From a single,
Unapproachable,
Still
Note.

Oh that we,
That we were there!
There,
Beyond this turning,
Beyond this folding,
And enfolding,
Of light in darkness,
And of sound in silence!

At Saint Mary Magdalene's

There is, after all,
Something—
An aspiration,
A longing,
A reaching out.
In these clouds
Of incense rising
Through crossed beams
Of winter light;
In these white tones
Rising, likewise, ethereal;
And in these acts,
Sanctioned by long age
As holy—
A cup lifted,
A knee bowed,
A gaze cast heavenward,
A gaze downcast
In a modesty of deacons,
And all along
The slow sad words
Of loss remembered,
And of gift unlooked for—
There is transfiguration,
Of a sort,
And a certain kind of peace.

A Garden, Walled

There's something about a wall,
The enclosure of
A secret garden,
That wants it up.

Here there is sanctuary,
A place to hide
From mundane business;
The protecting shade
Of the maple,
Its green, broad-arching dome,
Here the glossy veil of vines,
Here the ancient sounds
Of water in the fountain,
The arcane light,
Stolen,
By the gazing globe,
From an unsuspecting sky.

This is a place
For reconstructing
The garden lost,
For spiriting it back
From behind the angelic sword,
For walking,
In the cool of day,
In august company,
As heretofore.

This is a place for earthly delights,
For red-wine sherbet in crystal,
Gin in the cross-and-olive,
Or tea of Iran sucked,
As instructed,
Through lumps of sugar.

"My love," says Solomon,
"Is a garden, walled."

This is Where

And so it is here,
To this old Ontario town,
That we shall then come home.
Hand in hand we found it,
Giver of good gifts
By means of tea-shoppes,
By means of hills
And river valleys,
By means of an old church
Where clergy and old women
Danced on a-mazed grass,
And people whom we understood
Took us in,
And shared their grief and joy.
Therefore we live,
As then we too shall live,
In Hope.

Genealogy

Genealogy is the family pastime:

Grandad, at the cottage,
Answering, by lamplight,
Our questions
As we filled spaces
On the family tree,
Stopping us short,
Upright Rotarian that he was,
When we showed too much interest
In the myriad mystery persons—
The man stabbed to death
In the San Francisco Gold Rush!—
With "You wouldn't want to know.
He was a Poor Sort";

Aunt Alice, not even a Gray by birth,
Steeped in Gray family lore,
Deftly locating
A distant cousin's place
And lineage;

Daphne—on the Owen side—
Firmly passing down the word,
Via her most original daughter,
That "We certainly are not
Descended from a postmaster";

Miffy, up from the States,
Commanding a meeting of cousins
(On my cottage verandah)
To identify faces
In yellowing photographs.

We are all loremasters.
Let me show you.

Not here.
Come to the old city,
Where the buildings
And the places,
Have had time
To grow memories.

There!
Onto the top of that tower
My grandfather—
Yes, the faithful Rotarian
Who never missed a meeting
In fifty years,
Though I had to row him
Across the lake,
And drive him to Parry Sound;
Who ate oatmeal every day,
Though he "wouldn't say that he liked it"—
Hoisted a cow,
And was expelled
From the School of Practical Science.
The co-conspirator

Who never 'fessed up
(Mackenzie King)
Learned all too well
One of the practical sciences
His métier would require.

In that stained-glass window
Observe Aunt Gwynedd
As the Virgin Mary
Because she "looked so Jewish"
The artist said.

On that plaque
Read her brother's name:
Died in the war
From what recent revelations show
To have been "friendly" fire.
He studied here,
The family golden boy,
Already wounded
By older boys' abuse
At the boarding school
Run by Uncle Gore.
In love in England,
And with England—his diary tells me—
He and the others waited,
Endlessly,
Afraid to love
Or be loved,
Suspecting he had no future.
He left me only the borrowed memory
Of my first ice-cream cone.

There is his brother
On the wall,
And outside,
In the stonework,
The face of their father,
Smoking the endless fag ends
Of cigarettes
Stuffed in his mouth
By hungry undergraduates
Hurrying to dinner.

Here, in the church
Behind the Eaton Centre
Where my grandfather was rector,
My parents married,
And here they lived
In narrow Scadding House,
Carrying the dog
Down four flights of stairs,
My father pleased
Because the Scaddings
Were distant relatives by marriage,
The Scadding Cabin at the Ex
In some sense ours.

Here, off Alcina,
At the sign marked "Private Road"
Hides Wychwood Park,
Where my English great-grandparents
Settled at the end,
And scarcely knew
They were away.

Here—at the right time of year—
Off Bloor, and into the valley,
See a million scyllas
Descended from the twenty
Aunt Molly planted
When she was young, and hoped,
Before the bitterness
Captured her forever.

Not here, only,
Not in my personal memory only.

There are stories that lead
To the manor house in Wales,
Now demolished,
Though I saw it turned to flats,
And the formal garden
Still patterning
The overgrowth of weeds;

To the river up which
The Canniffs paddled
When they fled the Revolution,
The river on whose banks
They established their farms
And built their mills;

To New York,
And the British fleet,
And the resettlement
In Saint John;

To the canoe route
A ferocious ancestor took
With her seven children
Up through the Indian reservations
To Prince Edward County,
An ancestor so fierce
The man my parents hired
To cut the grass
Dared not stay and finish
Because her picture
Was "watching" him;

To Durham, and the captain's widow
Who joined her brothers in the new world
When his ship went down.

We are "old English Canadians"
Of course;
We don't often mention
Our Irish blood,
A distant Jewish ancestor
In England,
The Indian blood
That must be in our veins,
Or African,
For that matter,
When we,
Or some of us,
Had (and were)
West-Indian slaves.

We have been here
Long enough
To have no other homeland;
Long enough to mind
That others are inheriting—
Appropriating,
Demolishing—
All that once was ours.

Here I stand, then,
A conscious confluence
Of many rivers,
The brief efflorescence
Of a vast mycelium
Subterraneously stretching
To distant places,
Ancient times.

Here I stand,
Amongst the deracinated,
Those who are but of yesterday,
Lightly—
Unbearably lightly—
Unaware
Of the past that made them,
And in their unawareness
Blessed with an illusory freedom,
A freedom to which
I prefer
The richness
Of a tangled racination,

A landscape
Inhabited by ghosts,
And the rumours
Of what was,
Knowing who I am
By echolocation.

At 87

With an expectant smile,
She waits
For what life casts
Upon her shore.
The few small gifts
Time still holds in his hand
She will accept,
Hold up, with wonder,
To the light,
Love,
And gracefully let go.

Her Arms

"Oh, I am full of stories," she says.
Today it is the story of Geoffrey,
Who climbed into her lap—
Because she named my father—
And silently put his arms around her,
Knowing she must be grieving.

Little did she know
How soon his arms
Again would be around her,
The same arms that enfold Osiris,
The only great-grandchild,
The apple of her eye.

They are her arms:
They once enfolded me,
Through me enfolded Geoffrey,
And one day,
As Osiris's arms,
Will open to embrace
Whatever then is given him
To nurture and to love.

You Never Know

You never know,
When the telephone rings,
That it will not be:

A son
Calling collect
From a payphone on the street
To tell you of yet another betrayal
By the damaged young woman
He must someday learn
Not to love;

A son
Lately buoyed
By the confidence
He was charming the public,
Winning new custom
For his employers,
Achingly let go
On a consultant's
Ill-considered whim;

A daughter you knew
To be mismatched
With an inarticulate man,
But believed to be,
At least,
Safe with him forever,
Abandoned,
Four children
Distraught,
And him inarticulate
In this as in all else,
So that there is not even
The cold comfort
Of an explanation.

When we undertook
To be as gods
We didn't know
That in recreating ourselves
We gained immortality
In pain
As in all else,
And that,
If underneath
Are to be the everlasting arms,
Those arms,
Until our deaths,
Are ours,
And ours the hands
To wipe away,
Through our own tears,
The tears from our children's eyes.

The Shadow Children

We scarcely discern—
In the fierce, bright
Living of their siblings,
Irrefutably there
In the smell
And touch
And sound
Of their inescapably
Precious bodies—
The presence of
The shadow children,
Save as a dark halo
About the others' brightness,
Pointing at once
The miracle of their living,
The terror of their dying,
The burden that we bear
Of loving
In a place
Where none abides.

Briefing Notes

When it comes time
To write my epitaph,
Let it be said—
Not quite to the exclusion
Of all other words of praise—
That I have raised four sons,
Not one of whom will feel
That he has failed,
If he does not live up,
Or down,
To me.

Beyond

Three tiny cylinders
Do their level best
To propel you outwards,
Beyond the sprawling,
Topographically-challenged city,
Beyond the ageless, vapid,
Pudding face of the alluvial plain,
Beyond the first, flat horizon,
And its fabled endless sky.

You come to where the bones
Begin to show,
The skin to crease and fold,
To where the earth's face
Tells its own story—
Or keeps its secrets.

Yours the explorer's nose
To find them out,
The photographer's eye
For just how they can be drawn
Into the camera,
The anthropologist's attention
To how we have been there,
And to what we've left of ourselves
To stain the earth.

And the place itself,
Seeming to agree with Berkeley,
Knows itself to exist,
Again,
By being known.

Molly

Molly, the dragon-lady,
Eldest, and fiercest
Of my father's sisters,
Reducing to tears
The intended brides
Of brothers
And of nephews;
Impatient with her senile father,
Yet tender with the plants
She started in half-eggshells,
And planted out
In a bed she had nurtured fifty years
With tea-bags.

She worked, the rumour was,
In a lab—with eyes—
And was indispensable.

Witty, and caustic,
She was thoughtful with presents;
She favoured, shamelessly,
One nephew only—
A dubious distinction
None of us envied.

She was simply there,
The dragon on the hearth
Of the ancestral home,
Sharp, and dangerous,
And necessary
As the splinters
In the ancient hardwood floor
That we—forbidden—
Slid upon;
No one was surprised
To discover that she died—
In the narrow cot
In a corner of the nursery
She had never left—
Of malnutrition.

Ruth

When I laid her in Loyalist earth
By the cold St. Lawrence,
I remembered the way she entered
The Pine Hill living-room—
Drama,
And Rosalind Russell hair,
Upstaging us all,
Nieces, nephews,
The other maiden aunts
As—if the pictures do not lie—
She always had.

She was the Rosedale flirt,
With hundreds of boyfriends,
And not an inkling
Of what it was that happened,
On the wedding night,
Until my mother told her,
An appalled bride of fifty;

The Rosedale flirt who,
At sixty,
Nursed piglets at her fire,
As she nursed her chilblains,
In the ancient house
Where she heard
The children she had never had
Laughing in empty rooms.

When I last saw her living,
She thought I was my father,
And remembered
Our mother calling us
From the upstairs window.
Flirtatious to the end,
She offered a cheek,
Newly-plump
On nursing-home food:
"More to kiss"
She said

David

For a child who embraced decorum,
His mind filled
With stories of quiet English children
Tipping their hats,
Touching their forelocks,
Knowing their places,
Appalled if ever
They "attracted attention to themselves",
David was a burden.
"Hi Ruby!", "Hi Archie!"
He'd shout across the street
While I sat silent.

For sixty years,
His was the joyous voice
Greeting waitresses,
Ticket-takers,
George the janitor,
And Terry the archbishop,
All of whom knew,
For one brief moment at least,
That they were welcome.

When David died,
And silence fell,
Five hundred came
To mourn.

Cousins

Cousins—
Who needs them?
It's not as if you chose them,
Like friends.
They were just always there,
Part of the family landscape,
Like rocks and trees;
Irreducibly there,
In fact,
To be stumbled over at weddings,
Run into at funerals;
Inevitable as the extras
On a movie set.

Worse:
They have unfortunate memories
Of a you you had forgotten—
Or wished you could.
They've seen you naked,
Literally and—
Far worse—
Figuratively;
They know—
Let's say this outright—
Far too much.

Who needs them?
Well, you do.
Precisely because, not chosen,
They cannot choose to stop
Being there.
Precisely because,
When you need the long view
To grasp what's happening
In your life,
They have it.
Precisely because,
When you
And they
Fill full the glasses
And get down to drinking,
You're so far past embarrassment,
With them,
You tell the truth.
Precisely because,
Always being there,
They will be at your weddings,
And your funeral,
And will remember you.

A Cat's Lament for St. Valentine's Day

A sad day, St. Valentine's,
For a horticultural cat:
A dozen long-stemmed roses
Wasting their substance
On the desert air
Of a locked bedroom,
Forbidden to me
Who love them passionately—
As passionately as does she
To whom,
In error,
They were sent.

Boad

Oh! Did I wake you?
You stroke me; I'll purr.
That should help you sleep.

Gratuity

Though it was the customary place
For such petitions,
I could not ask
That I be spared—
Not because I did not long,
And not because I did not fear;
Could not ask, even,
"Why me?"
When it seemed so obvious
The real question
Was "Why not me?"—
To which I knew no answer.

When I was spared,
All I could do
Was stand with open hands,
The lucky victim
Of inscrutable grace,
Recipient of a gift
Unlooked-for,
And unearned.

Beyond the Apogee

When we were children
We pumped and pumped the swings
Until,
At maximum arc,
We parted ways
And,
Carried for a moment
By that slight momentum,
We rose still further,
Hung, deliciously,
Weightless,
As if this were our natural state
And we the inhabitants of air
And flight,
Delirious conquerors of the gravity
Inherent in our mass,
(Directly proportionate,
Distance squared, etc.)
Just before the fall that waits
Beyond the apogee.

Now, at this age,
We,
Kin to those stars they speak of
"Wobbling" at the transit
Of distant planets
Sister to our own,
Or—worse—
Like galaxies
Spinning in
Vast,
Unimaginable
Vortices
Into the yet more unimaginable
Densities
Known only as black holes,
Know ourselves, too, to be
Beyond the apogee.

It Seems, Then

It seems, then,
That the God who loved
The bowl of sculptured snow
About a dark tree
In the blizzard of '43,
The yellow of old brick
At Church Street,
The deep purple-blue
Of snow beneath my skis
At the end of that winter's day
By the huddle of cedars,
And the first green of willows
By the Don Valley Parkway,
Signalling Spring,

Loves, too,
The reek of kerosene,
The clunk of landing-wheels upraised,
The roar of GE engines—
Tickling with turbulence
The fragile fuselage
In which I ride—
Cherishes the HI viruses
That safely graze,
And one day will approve
The deep crimson
Of one small, dying star,
As we approve
A glowing cigarette,
Beautifying
The all-surrounding dark

Asters

"The royal purple," Theodora said,
"Doth make a splendid winding-sheet."

And so it does:
The earth, death-bound,
Is swathed in bands of aster,
Amethyst set in gold
Of black-eyed susans
And of goldenrod,
Proclaiming thereby,
To winter's face,
The royal worth
Of seasons passing,
And dropping,
Surreptitiously,
On darkening ground
The last, cold-ripened seeds,
Against the king's return.

Acknowledgements

The Sounds of Ice, With My Father at the Symphony, Finding the Tao, Thrust the Dark, Blue Blade, and *In One Another's Eyes* first appeared in *A View on the Garden* VII (1998) on pages 10, 13, 15, 16, and 17 respectively.

Ruth, and *A Garden, Walled* first appeared in *A View on the Garden* VIII (2000) pages 37 and 38 respectively.

Red-Wing and *Spring Gold* first appeared in *A View on the Garden* IX (2002), pp. 52 and 53 respectively.

You Never Know first appeared in *A View on the Garden* X (2003) on pages 22–23.

A Biographical Sketch of Patrick T. R. Gray

Born in Toronto in 1940, and growing up in Markham, Patrick has lived almost all of his life in southern Ontario, whose fields, forests, and lakes he loves. He currently lives in active retirement in Port Hope, though he spends a good deal of time as well at his cottage on Pigeon Lake. He is blissfully married to Cathy Carlyle, to whom in gratitude this collection is dedicated, and is the father of four sons, the stepfather of a daughter and two more sons, and grandfather indiscriminately of an increasing number of children.

As he relates in the preface, Patrick's love for poetry began when he was read A. A. Milne and Beatrix Potter in the nursery, and was transformed by hearing Dylan Thomas reading such poems as *Do Not Go Gentle into that Good Night*, and *Fern Hill*.

Over the years he dabbled occasionally in poetry, but it was only in the last dozen or so years, beginning with a difficult sojourn on Amherst Island in Lake Ontario, that his poetic creative urge came into spate, the collection *This Grace of Light* being the first serious published result. He participated in the Atkinson College (York University)

Writers at Noon poetry group, and more recently in the Cobourg Poetry Workshop, each of which provided both a stimulus to write and a sympathetic audience.

For the rest, Patrick had a day job as a university professor of theology and religious studies, teaching at the University of Toronto, McMaster, and York, in which capacity he published numerous academic articles, mostly on fifth- and sixth-century theological disputes, one book, *The Defense of Chalcedon in the East (451-553)*, and an edition and translation, *Leontius of Jerusalem, Against the Monophysites*. He continues to do research and to disseminate it at conferences; he plans at least one further academic book, this one on the exploitation of Cyril of Alexandria's status as an arbiter of orthodoxy. He also assisted in various church congregations as an Anglican priest, as he does currently at St. Mark's Anglican Church in Port Hope. He is proud of his abilities as a home winemaker, honed over almost five decades of sometimes disastrous experimentation.

Other books in the North Shore Series

Find full information at
– http://www.HiddenBrookPress.com/b-NShore.html

First set of five books

— **M.E. Csamer** – Kingston – "A Month Without Snow"
  – Prose – ISBN – 978-1-897475-87-2
— **Elizabeth Greene** – Kingston – "The Iron Shoes"
  – Poetry – ISBN – 978-1-897475-76-6
— **Richard Grove** – Brighton – "A Family Reunion"
  – Prose – ISBN – 978-1-897475-90-2
— **R.D. Roy** – Trenton – "A Pre emptive Kindness"
  – Prose – ISBN – 978-1-897475-80-3
— **Eric Winter** – Cobourg – "The Man In The Hat"
  – Poetry – ISBN – 978-1-897475-77-3

Second set of five books

— **Janet Richards** – Belleville – "Glass Skin"
  – Poetry – ISBN – 978-1-897475-01-0
— **R.D. Roy** – Trenton – "Three Cities"
  – Poetry – ISBN – 978-1-897475-96-4
— **Wayne Schlepp** – Cobourg – "The Darker Edges of the Sky"
  – Poetry – ISBN – 978-1-897475-99-5
— **Benjamin Sheedy** – Kingston – "A Centre in Which They Breed"
  – Poetry – ISBN – 978-1-897475-98-8
— **Patricia Stone** – Peterborough – "All Things Considered"
  – Prose – ISBN – 978-1-897475-04-1

Third set of five books

— **Mark Clement** – Cobourg – "Island In the Shadow"
  – Poetry – ISBN – 978-1-897475-08-9
— **Anthony Donnelly** – Brighton – "Fishbowl Fridays"
  – Prose – ISBN – 978-1-897475-02-7
— **Chris Faiers** – Marmora – "ZenRiver Poems & Haibun"
  – Poetry – ISBN – 978-1-897475-25-6
— **Shane Joseph** – Cobourg – "Fringe Dwellers" *Second Edition*
  – Prose – ISBN – 978-1-897475-44-7
— **Deborah Panko** – Cobourg – "Somewhat Elsewhere"
  – Poetry – ISBN – 978-1-897475-13-3

Forth set of five books

— **Diane Dawber** – Bath – "Driving, Braking and Getting out to Walk"
  – Poetry – ISBN – 978-1-897475-40-9
— **Patric Gray** – Port Hope – "This Grace of Light"
  – Poetry – ISBN – 978-1-897475-34-8
— **John Pigeau** – Kingston – "The Nothing Waltz"
  – Prose – ISBN – 978-1-897475-37-9
— **Mike Johnston** – Cobourg – "Reflections Around the Sun"
  – Poetry – ISBN – 978-1-897475-38-6
— **Kathryn MacDonald** – Shannonville – "Calla & Édourd"
  – Prose – ISBN – 978-1-897475-39-3

Single Anthology

"**Changing Ways**" A book of prose by Cobourg area authors including: Jean Edgar Benitz, Patricia Calder, Fran O'Hara Campbell, Leonard D'Agostino, Shane Joseph, Brian Mullally. **Editor: Jacob Hogeterp**
— ISBN – 978-1-897475-22-5

www.ingramcontent.com/pod-product-compliance
Lightning Source LLC
Chambersburg PA
CBHW021120080526
44587CB00010B/580